Memories, Thoughts, and Dreams

Memories, Thoughts, and Dreams

Follow on guybalapoet.blogspot.com

"LIKE" FB
Memories, Thoughts, and Dreams

Guy Bala

Copyright © 2012 by Guy Bala.

Library of Congress Control Number:		2012909222
ISBN:	Hardcover	978-1-4771-1591-6
	Softcover	978-1-4771-1590-9
	Ebook	978-1-4771-1592-3

All rights reserved. No part of this book may be reproduced or transmitted in any form or by any means, electronic or mechanical, including photocopying, recording, or by any information storage and retrieval system, without permission in writing from the copyright owner.

2nd printing 2012
Includes the epic poem
"A Mountains' Sojourn"
Originally published in *The Highlander,* September 4, 2001

This book was printed in the United States of America.

To order additional copies of this book, contact:
Xlibris Corporation
1-888-795-4274
www.Xlibris.com
Orders@Xlibris.com

I have met everyone in my life for some
Reason or another . . . . I know.
I've gone back, reflected and pondered.
Fate, destiny, fortune, or providence.
Each and every one of you.
A life experience whether
Simply something learned,
Something loved, or perhaps something lost.
Grateful for each and every one.
Hopefully, in turn, I have been
A muse, a mentor, an inspiration
For all of you that my life has touched.

ACKNOWLEDGEMENTS

As I prepare this book for publication, I am reminded of the many people who have passed through my life and gifted me with experiences, positive and not-so-positive, that are reflected in this book of poems. For me, poetry is a language that has the most appropriate wording and structure that allows me to express myself. It is a language that most easily encases what I am feeling. The poetry that fills these pages began rather innocently, with scribbles of words, then lines and phrases, scratched on cocktail napkins and the odd scraps of paper. After a while, a pattern began to emerge, like a musical score come to life, a performance of dance brought to movement, or an inspiring landscape swashed across a canvas. It became clear that my heart had things to say.

Yet, poetic inspiration and flowery verse are not the primary reason for my writing this book. Rather, my reasons for self-expression are about the reflections one catches of oneself when one's relationships hold up the necessary and appropriate mirrors for self-exploration. I believe this is how we come to understand ourselves, and in doing so, come to understand one another.

While the writing occurs in quiet solitude, the experiences of creation are full of breadth, encompassing many people who contribute their time and expertise, and most importantly, their belief in the work. The following people are a part of my journey in creating the poetry of *Memories, Thoughts, and Dreams*. I have been truly fortunate in their participation in my life and in my work, both artistically and professionally. They deserve a special acknowledgement for their unique contributions.

Thank you to my publisher, XLIBRIS, for affording me this wonderful dream of sharing my book with the world. Your team support has been incredible and I really appreciate all the attentive TLC you have shown me as a newly published writer.

Thank you to my editor, Shannan Anderson, for her special talent in teaching me to always be aware of the reader, to consider how others may view what I am trying to express, and to understand that sometimes what I write isn't necessarily what the reader reads — one must always have respect for the reader! This is a critical distinction to make and I am very grateful for such insight.

Thank you to my staff, my colleagues, and the hundreds of volunteers who worked with me and for me at the Broward Center for the Performing Arts. We shared a wonderfully dedicated interest in the arts, and you have left an indelible sense of the importance of collaboration on my professional psyche. I am also very grateful for the thousands of patrons who supported our work and in the pleasure I had in coming to personally know so many of them.

And a special thank you to my dearest friends and family for their continued support and enthusiasm for my life's journey and this book of poetry. They all know that I love and cherish them deeply.

In Remembrance

My parents Stanley and Rose Marie Bala and my brother Luke; My special friend, Sandy, never giving up, lived a generous and loving life, fighting with great determination, courage, and strength, until succumbing to ovarian cancer.

GB

On the web at *www.guybala.com*

INTRODUCTION

Love! Is there anything more important in life? Shakespeare, Schubert, Byron, Brahms, Keats, Shelley, and Browning all produced historical odes to love! Some were comedic, some were maudlin, some were ironic and sarcastic, and others poignant to the point of tears. Add to this body of love reflections, Guy Bala's small, but beautiful little collection, *Memories, Thoughts, and Dreams*. In this poetic work, Bala has crafted a prismatic gem in which simple and genuine feelings of love and loss, and love again are laid bare for reflection. Bala's verse reveals a full spectrum of a poet's innermost feelings, accompanied with splendid imagery, and expressions of great beauty. Anyone who has experienced the miracle of life, love, and loss will find their feelings expressed simply, yet eloquently in Bala's moving, empathetic, and melancholic verse. Bala's experience is often raw on the page, as he writes in a most genuine and reflective style. Such pared-to-the-core honesty pulls the reader quickly into experiences that are universally shared.

Memories, Thoughts, and Dreams poses the question, although it is never directly asked . . . Is there a rational explanation for the force of love? Bala, the poet answers, "No, there is no rhyme nor reason in the loving of another human being and being loved in return . . . other than, this miracle provides our utmost reason for living, for thinking, for dreaming, and for reflection. A heart unexamined neither understands love nor realizes when it passes through." Bala's verses gives us pause to reflect on what should be our greatest purpose in life, regardless of what ultimate sorrow may come, and that is to love and be loved. That Bala should produce such a poetic little gem should come as no surprise considering his artistic background in dance and choreography. Understanding the need to move with fluidity easily translates into admonishings that one must take the chance on love, even when all hope seems a futile endeavor . . . still one must commit to love.

Memories, Thoughts, and Dreams encourages us to remember, to recall a time when we were head-over-heels in new love. It also reminds us of the poignancy that sleeps in our memories of a love lost.

B K Shaw

TABLE OF CONTENTS

A MOUNTAIN'S SOJOURN 1

A LIFE'S SOJOURN 6

WHAT IS BEAUTY? 7

BEAUTY IS 8

THE BEAUTY OF YOU 9

THE FLOWER 10

YET 11

SILENCE 14

MY LIFE 15

JUST THE TWO OF US 16

LOVE 17

LOVING YOU 18

THE ART OF LOVE 19

AT LONG LAST US 20

BEFORE THE WORLD 21

MY WORLD 22

TODAY 23

THE KISS	24
IF ONLY	26
SEARCHING	27
SOMEONE ELSE	28
WHAT ONCE WAS	29
I LOVED YOU	30
SOMETHING, SOMEONE	31
WALKING	32
HER LOVE WAS MY LIFE	33
THE ONE I FOUND	34
ALONE	36

A MOUNTAIN'S SOJOURN

Originally Published
In The Highlander
Highlands, N.C.
September 4, 2001

A Mountain's Sojourn

Leaves change color and trees evolve
As we watch the wonder of fall.
Green, the backdrop as a single leaf,
Fades and dissolves from color to color.
One tree shares pale yellows,
Golden oranges and rust reds
Another a yellow rose, rusty orange
And mahogany red,
Yet another bathed in sun-kissed ginger.
Our eyes leaf through, scanning
The mountainsides,
The forest is lush and vivid with
The hues of a luxuriant painting.
Colors bursting and flashing in and out of focus,
Autumn leaves pour out of their trees raining, And
dropping from still branches
Drifting, falling, and twisting
Toward the ground.
Resting there and at times,
Whirling into wind-swept swirls.

Winter begins, rain with tiny beads of
Snow held in each bubble,
Expanding and wrapping around the
Droplets of rain, becoming, evolving into huge White
flakes, drifting, floating, and dropping.

The air is silent save for the soft swirling,
Twirling of a weighty flake of snow.

Quietly, silently, a blanket takes shape,
Snow embraces the ground.

Trees become stark under limbs
Coarse and charcoal gray.

In the clear of the brittle icy night
Bright white snow crusts over each
Branch and crook.
Crisp clear skies, with stars shining
So bright and luminous,
Overflow the sky, reaching mountain slopes.
Starlight freckles twinkle from lit
Windowed houses,
Appearing magically through winter
Barren branches.

A second snow masks the earth, the cold settles in,
Ponds freeze in artic air.
The world turns quiet, creating a profound
Silence, soundlessness, muffled and muted.
The night is hushed and noiseless,
With a bright and radiant moon
Glistening on the blanketed ground,
Fabricating a dazzling, shimmering, carpet.
Inside on this winter night, a fire burns
Uplifting, cheerful, soothing, and relaxing
Losing ourselves in the licking, flicking flames,
Undulating reds, oranges, blues, and greens.
Flames sensuously massaging the logs of wood
Flames with caverns, crevices, and peaks,
Flames with tongues intertwining,
Dancing and embracing,
Embers breathe and pulsate.
A breath rising in the smoke, a heart beating
Within the fiery and consuming blaze.
Heat emanates and radiates, and hypnotically
We are drawn into the heat of
A concert being played by the devouring fire.
Outside the night is cold and frigid
The fire within is warm and soothing.

Early morning appears with sharp,
Clear blue skies.
A light, crisp morning breeze flutters through the
Barren branches of the forest trees.

Morning marches into the noonday, clouds
Appear, dotting the crystalline sky.
The breeze heightens, continuing its
Journey from the north.
Hours pass as the atmosphere unfolds and swells,
The temperature plunges.
Dusk approaches, the wind and clouds stall and
Halt over the mountain peaks.
Ominously, clouds bond, growing
Gloomy and heavy,
Heavy with winter's moisture descending ever
Downward onto the summits,
Night brings a howling wind, thundering and
Threatening, through the mountain gorge.

The sky darkens beyond the night,
Obscuring the mountains.
Blackened firmament and towering
Land masses become one.
Snow cascades as winter reawakens and the
Wind sustains its course.
Snow, light at first, then with a heavy
Determination, demonstrates its
Silent and vast power.
Through the night, the snow persists,
Accumulating until finally light
Seeps through the obscured heavens.
Morning brings a shiver and a somberly
Muted glow as the last flakes of
Winter rain drift ever downward.
The sun, a faint disk, appears
Resembling a full and rounded moon.
Finally, stillness settles across the slopes
And valleys, as the snow ends.

As winter retreats, the quiet is no longer.
Life is resounding all about us.
Spring begins with birds and bees
Singing and buzzing in a freshly scented morn
Butterflies flutter as the warm air
Soaks into the ground.

Magically, buds appear on
Twigs, sprigs, and trees,
Creamy whites, soft greens, pastel yellows,
Delicate pinks, and faint reds.
Blink an eye and buds bloom, and flowers
Assail the hillside slopes.
The earth's bouquet awakens our senses
To breathe in the scent of spring, of rebirth
Longer days recede into cheerful dusks
As insects begin their chirping.
Night brings out croaking pond frogs,
And whispering whippoorwills.

As days go by, blooms blossom and flowers
Mature brightly, vivid and vibrant.
Spring melts itself into summer
And the alpine rain forest changes once more.
Mornings are alive with puffy, cottony clouds
Dotting the deep, royal blue dell.
The sun arcs itself from eastern mountain ridges,
Traversing a translucent sky.
Clouds stall and meld themselves into each
Other, building and growing heavily.
Suddenly rain emanates from the soaked clouds
And descends downward, earth bound.
Waterfalls spring over cliffs and rocks; creeks rage
On with sounds of rushing water,
Relentlessly surging into overflowing ponds.
The strangled croaks of frogs are heard as the
Gulley-washing deluge recedes.
The earth overflows with muskiness, an earthen
Ripeness, bursts in summer's upwelling renewal.
The suns of summer march through new blooms,
New blossoms never ceasing.
Valleys and hillsides are richly puckered,
Puffed, and quilted.
Greens of every shade and texture become
A living background to the splashes and
Wisps of pigments.
Ever new additions of colorful hues dramatize a
Spectrum of light variation.

New found shades dabble on the crests of
Hillsides, blinking through the forest
And sweeping over the shallows of the meadows,

A living, breathing
And ever changing landscape.
Warm rains pour through forest trees
Soaking into the lush earth.
Summer wears on, the sun rises high,
And wild berries taste flush and robust.

And time and seasons return yet again to the
Mountain's sojourn of passing,
One season to another, one adventure to
Another, and one life to another.

A LIFE'S SOJOURN

The beauty of living, of loving
The wonder of grasping what surrounds me
Follows me harmoniously,
Traveling with me as my journey goes on.

It's a journey of time, a journey through life.
A sojourn of seasons passing all around me,
The beauty of each spring,
Summer, fall and winter.
The wonder of life, the miracle of
Love and beauty.

I wonder at the beauty of it all.
The beauty that I see,
The beauty that I feel,
The world,
The people,
All around me.

It's all so natural
Yet so surreal.
So magical
Yet so genuine,
As if everything around me
Can't be, but is.
Through time and the seasons,
Traveling through life
And the seasons of love.

WHAT IS BEAUTY?

What is Beauty?
A day of sun
A night of fun
A flower's scent so sweet
A life lived so complete.

What is Beauty?
Eyes glowing
Lips smiling
A tender caress
A kiss no less.

What is Beauty?
Holding hands
Wedding bands
The number two
Most of all . . .

You

BEAUTY IS

I thought of you today.
I pictured you
Such a Flower among flowers.
No garden can compare
Such beauty among beauty.
No garden is as lovely

    . . . you are what beauty is.

THE BEAUTY OF YOU

Ah !
My chance to be alone
My time to think
My mind is peaceful
My soul serene

Ah !
Tonight I sensed beauty
Tonight my heart fluttered
Tonight my eyes beheld
Tonight my arms embraced

Ah !
Beauty above beauty
Beauty
Beauty all of her own
Beauty
Beauty of You
Beauty
Beauty for me alone

THE FLOWER

I am a flower
and
You could be a flower.
But then . . .
You are so much more.

YET

You hold me in your arms
      Yet
You wish I were not real.
You kiss me with your lips
      Yet
You wish we had never met.
You touch my soul with yours
      Yet
You wish we were never one.
You love me with your heart
      Yet
You wish it were not so.

            I lay in your arms
                  Yet
            I wish it were only a dream.
            I taste your lips
                  Yet
            I wish they were not so sweet.
            I feel our souls embracing
                  Yet
            I wish I had no soul.
            I love you with all my heart
                  Yet
            I am afraid to love.

And this . . .

. . . this is love

SILENCE

We need no words
Our eyes speak
Our touch reveals

In silence we search
In silence we find

Words without meaning
Tenderness beyond our dreams

In silence we discover

I you, and you I

Knowing without saying
Understanding without explaining

'Sorry' and 'love' are words no longer
A touch, a glance, a caress
Speak for you and I

In silence we discover each other.

MY LIFE

I need not have been born
I have no desire,
Nor any need to exist.
The hour, the place, the way
After birth
I need now only to die;
I desire it so.

The touch of your hand
Tender, warm, loving
Kindles within my soul
The will to live
I need now only to die;
I desire it not.

Give me my life.
Preserve the thought I am.
I have no past,
The future is not mine.
The hour I cherish,
The place I love,
The way I need
Is now
With you
In silent love.
Then I may die
My soul living

. . . forever.

JUST THE TWO OF US

Just the two of us
We walk, we talk
Strolling through nature
Undisturbed by the world.
A hushed breeze travels through
Half barren limbs.

Just the two of us
The gentle, brisk breeze
Caresses our faces
Fluttering leaves embrace our legs.

Just the two of us
We romp and run
Gloved hands touch
Bundled arms encase bundled bodies.
A branch snaps underfoot
Dry lips crack into a smile
Bright, searching eyes
Cold, red noses
Nature, us
We love
You and I.

LOVE

My life has changed.
Time is not as it once was.
The hours have expanded.
The days have lengthened.

>   Rising in the east, the sun
>   Is now a blessing I hold dearly.
>   Setting in the west, the sun
>   With all its beauty reflects my day.
>   My nights are restless
>   Only exhausted can I sleep.
>   My mind races and dreams.
>
>   I am no longer myself
>   I myself am not enough
>   I am a part of much more

Together with you

>   . . . I am complete.

LOVING YOU

All my love, my special Lady
All my life for you I live.
Alive for you, my mornings are bright
Loving you, my days are breath-taking
All my life, my nights never ending
All my love for you, my special Lady, I so live.

My precious Lady, all my love
For you, I love all my life.
Your smile brings me to life, alive for you
Loving to live, loving life, loving you.
Without you, I would have no life
For you, my precious Lady, I so give all my love.

All my love, all my life, my special Lady
All my life, all my love, my precious Lady
Alive for you, alive for your smile
Loving you, loving your smile
All my life, all my days, all my nights
All my love, to live is loving you.

All my love
All my life
Alive for you
Loving you
All my life
All my love

The ART OF LOVE

I am, you are.
We are, you and I.
We touch.
My fingertips brush you,
Painting you.
Brush strokes, the tips of my fingers
The canvas of your skin.
Your fingers mirror mine
Caressing the canvas of my skin
Painting me.

Our brushes change.
From just moistened fingertips
To warmer, softened lips,
And tips of pliant tongues.
Our breaths become the paint,
Our moans the foreground.
A work of art thriving and flourishing.
We become alive, alive within the painting.
Alive in life, in living, and loving.
Our passion comes to life
You and I living and loving
Vibrant and alive, loving each other
Loving and living as the art of love.

AT LONG LAST US

Morning has dawned.
The sun, rising in the east,
Kisses the dew-covered grass.
The birds sing out a welcome
To a new born day.

This morning I am alone
Alone more than any other morning.
Time passes slowly
More slowly than time has ever passed.

Today is a day of many days.
You stand alone.
I stand alone waiting.
For in time our lives will change.

Night has fallen
The sun, setting in the west,
Glows with the warmth of our love.
You and I are no longer alone
Together we shall welcome a newborn day.

BEFORE THE WORLD

Look back to each yesterday
Each beautiful day.
Not one can compare
To the beauty of today.
Yet today is just the beginning
The joy of each day which follows
Will nouridsh the love
We witness beween you.

And now, you stand
Hand in hand
Before the world.
Your lives grow richer.
As we listen to your love
A love whch begins deeper
Than we can ever imagine,
A love which only you
Together
Will come to know.

MY WORLD

Your tender hand I gently take
And hold within my grasp
The sunshine of my world.

You shine your light
Into my darkness.
You caress me
With your warmth.

As life itself needs the sun,
You are the sun I need,
The light I desire,
The warmth I love.

My sun.   My world.   My love.

TODAY

Today was no different
Than any other day.
Yesterday . . .
It was but a tomorrow.
And tomorrow . . .
It will be no more
Than a yesterday.

Today I thought of you
As I do any other day.
Thoughts of love
Thoughts of you and I.

Today I dreamt of you
As I do any other day.
Dreams of passion
Dreams of you and I.

Today, Yesterday, Tomorrow
There is no difference.
They are always
You and I.

THE KISS

Sometimes it's forgotten,
So long ago, forgotten.
Yet there is something,
Something that can't be forgotten
Yet, not quite remembered.
Not because it was forgotten, but
Because this kiss was never repeated
With anyone else.

That first kiss so long ago,
That eternal kiss that we shared.
Kiss after kiss after kiss
Never replaced by another.
Years go by and in years gone by
It can't be remembered,
Something so special.
Lips touching each other's
Warm and inviting, but so much more.

So tender and giving
Yours taking mine
As mine takes yours.
It's the breath
We shared.

The breath of it, the
Softness yet intensity of it.
Lips pressing more gently,
Yet wanton in the depth
The sensousness of it
Tender, yet demanding.

It's the kiss that only
You and I shared.
That kiss so long ago
That I can only remember.
Now as our lips touch
Once again from so long ago.

IF ONLY

if only my mind were
able to see,
to see as easily as my
eyes
to hear,
to hear as easily as my
ears
to feel,
to feel as easily as my
hands . . .

Maybe then
I could understand.

SEARCHING

*Fair wind
Tell me
What is it that you know?
The brilliance of the sunrise,
The peace of the sunset.
At night
The soft glowing moon casts shadows
Stars flicker, brightly, faintly.*

   I need knowledge of more.

*Fair wind
The sun, the moon, the stars
They have their course.
They need not know their direction.
They serve without question.*

   I must question.

*Fair wind
My strength, my mind, my being
Their direction is unknown.
What is my course
To do, to think, to believe.*

   *Can you hear?
   Answer my being.*

SOMEONE ELSE

She wanted love
But not mine.
Love from before
A love she had no more.

WHAT ONCE WAS

I once had a friend
Living life, sharing life
Loving life, together.

Then my friend was no more.
My friend died. I'm crying,
Existing, hating life, alone.

I mourned for my friend.

My friend is gone
I must forget what once was.
Live again, share again,
Love again.

I must, bury what has died
At any cost, I must try.

For life and love, can only be mine
If I can free myself from

              . . . what once was.

I LOVED YOU

How many times have I,
How many times
Have I loved you?
I have loved you many times
Many times I have loved you.

I close my eyes to see you.
I close my eyes to touch you.
Whenever I open my eyes
My eyes cry for you.
I open my eyes and I miss you.

Whenever I am asleep
You are with me.
You reach out your hand to me
You give me your love.
I awake and find I am alone.

Once you were here
Whether my eyes were opened or closed.
Once you were real
Whether awake or asleep.
Once you were mine.

How many times have I,
How many times
Have I loved you?
I loved you many times
Many times I loved you.

SOMETHING, SOMEONE

The wind is brisk against me.
The vibrating branches speak.
Yet I cannot understand.
I turn To face the wind.

Tell me, What is it that you know?
Say something. I will listen
For I am in need of
Something, Someone,

To know
And to love.

WALKING

My steps are light
I walk without purpose.
Rather
I wander without meaning
The park is full today.

Without emotion, I watch
People
Together
Playing
Couples
Together, sharing
Life surrounds me.

They see me
A passing shadow.
Perhaps
As the past they dread,
Or maybe
The future they fear.
They shun me
I shun them.

My world is my own.
Others live in a dimension
I am unable to find.
I walk no more,
I stop
No longer existing.

HER LOVE WAS MY LIFE

To be alive, yet not living
To exist for eternity knowing
Life will never be mine.

To have had a life
To have lost that life
To know the joy of life
Realizing the joy I will never have again.

Each day the pain, the sorrow grows.
Each day wanting life more than the last.
Each night hating myself for losing my life.

Breathing reminds me of life,
Being causes endless pain.

I would gladly give my life
To have her love once more.

THE ONE I FOUND

Behold the silence,
See the purity,
Embrace the beauty,
A blanket, a pillow,
A shroud of serenity, of peace
Whiteness as no other.

Brightness beyond any other,
Warm as the sun, cold as the ice,
Snow beautiful and bright.
I reach out my hand,
I have found a flake,
Which is more than snow.

It holds more than beauty,
Alone it surpasses the blanket.
Clinging to the flake, the flake touching me
But for no more than a brief moment.
It will not allow me to hold, to cherish what it is.
I have lost the one thing I found.

I shall never find a flake
of snow
As the one I
found
Cherished and
lost.

ALONE

I have been
Lost too long

Lost

Among the people
Crowded but

Alone

In my agony
Lost, alone

Searching for,
Someone

I need to hold
To be held

Where are
You

Maybe there isn't

Anyone,
No one

Only
Me

Forever
Alone

ABOUT THE AUTHOR

Guy Bala has been called a renaissance man, a bon vivant, an epicurean, and a modern-day bohemian, and rightly so—for such descriptions fit him well. Inspired by the "unsanctioned poets" of his youth—Bob Seeger, Journey, Foreigner, Styx, Fleetwood Mac and the Moody Blues, to name a few, Bala recognized early on the critical importance of *artistic interpretation*. Although an ardent fan of all traditional models of literature, Bala believes poetry to have an immediate and universal recognition of human emotions. "Words used everyday take on a profound simplicity. They become lyrical and stay in our minds, like music. Indeed, poetry often produces the most emotive sensibilities that strike at our hearts. We share universal experiences, no matter who we are or where we live. Our interpretations are different, and yet the same."

Bala is a sensitive observer of humanity and his observations are reflected in his work. "I am intrigued with humanity. The art of being a human is something that fascinates me . . . those things that make living a shared experience . . . the colorful palette of emotional capabilities to express what one thinks and feels. For me, these border on the ethereal."

With an extensive background in the theatrical arts, particularly music, dance and choreography, it is no surprise that Bala seeks to express his feelings with the same artistic elements of movement and fluidity. He finds the poetic form the perfect medium of self-expression. "The beauty of poetry is this—it is sublimely aligned with the same inherent flow of movement, of rhythm, and lyricism found in dance and music. It is also pure in expression. There is an honesty to poetry that flows from mind to heart. That is the power of the art form."

In his latest work, *Memories, Thoughts, and Dreams*, Bala reveals a sweet sensitivity that speaks sincerely of love, loss, and loneliness. "I'm not afraid to reflect on my experiences and excavate my thoughts concerning them. It's how I have come to understand myself."

A Michigan Dearbornite, Guy Bala began his performance work as a circus acrobat. From there, he quickly advanced to teaching gymnastics and choreographing performance pieces of various genres for his students. He has appeared in a variety of staged musicals as principle dancer, Fiddler on the Roof, Applause, Mame, Follies, and the King and I, to name a few. He later studied modern ballet in Royal Oak, Michigan and also studied and performed with the Ann Arbor Civic Ballet.

While living on the beaches of SE FL, Bala was engaged in 1991 to spearhead the recruitment and training of one of the largest professional (upwards of 800 active) volunteer corps in the U.S. at the Broward Center of the Performing Arts in Ft. Lauderdale, Florida. He interlocked a mission of impacting the love of the arts with the necessary hospitality nature required to successfully service as many as 25,000 weekly patrons. During this tenure, he also produced a documentary, *The Birth of an Arts Center*, depicting the anticipation and suspense of the Broward Center's premier performance as they grandly opened with *The Phantom of the Opera*.

Following the Broward Center tenure, Bala then moved to a time and place of quiet reflectiveness. He settled in Highlands, North Carolina, within the Nantahala National Forest. Here he introduced a poetry reading program, "Poets at the Podium," for the Bascom Center for the Visual Arts. He also wrote "A Mountain's Sojourn" which was published in the Highlander on September 4th 2001.

Today, Bala resides in Tampa, Florida with his two rescues, Aki and Rafiki. When not working on his next artistic venture, he can be found in the kitchen, crafting a new gourmet dish. A true bon vivant!

CPSIA information can be obtained at www.ICGtesting.com
Printed in the USA
BVOW011945201112

306073BV00002B/1/P